All rights Reserved.
© GRAHAM OSMENT

ISBN. 1 898964 00 9

First published 1994 by

ORCHARD
PUBLICATIONS

2, Orchard Close, Chudleigh, Newton Abbot, Devon TQ13 0LR.
Tel: (0626) 852714

Front cover and illustrations by
Brian Steffens

All rights reserved. No part of this publication may be reproduced, stored in a retrieval system, or transmitted in any form or by any means, without the prior permission of the copyright holder.

To Dad

ಬಆಬಆಬಆಬಆ

VARMYARD UNI-VERSE-ITY

by

Graham Osment

ಬಆಬಆಬಆಬಆ

FOREWORD

Last year Graham approached my colleague, Janette Leitch, and myself for advice about developing his writing. We read the samples he'd brought along and were immediately captivated by their freshness and humour. Graham's poems are a robust celebration of the life of old Devon, delivered in the authentic and fast disappearing local dialect. He has a shrewd eye for detail, a fine ear for dialogue, and a talent for making his characters spring to life from the page.

Janette's advice to Graham was "Get a word processor", and mine was "Get a publisher!" We are pleased to see that he's done both, and wish him great success with this, his first volume of poetry.

Elaine Towns

Foreword	ii
Time	5
Me New Vriend	6
Shoud Us Keep A Cow	8
Varmer 'Cross The Valley	12
Swede Puller Grade 1	13
Jack Luckmen	16
Vus Day Uv Zhearen	18
Zcwib's Torch	21
Chapel	23
Brither's Pride	26
I've Ad A Belly Vull	29
All-Uz On A Zunday	34
Me Old Man's Draven	36
Dancen	38
Death Ally	40
Reubin's Lament	42
Tez Only Temporary	44
Deb'n Dialect Verse	46
Glossary	48

TIME

I stood and watched through the years
watched the atmospheric life of folk so full
of pride.
Real people who toil with hand that love their
land so grand.

Fed my soul trained my hand allowed the eye
to watch.
How to thank those gone before
and care for treasure left behind
To do justice to their time.

So with verse I will remember, convey
it from the heart,
a tribute for and to,
I feel them coming through.

The farmer, the vet, shearer, worker, miller
all in part there from the start.
My Dear Father with great character depart
I feed the verse to tell the story and the glory.

ME NEW VRIEND

ಬಂಡಬಂಡಬಂಡಬಂಡ

I've voun a vreind to elp me, write these lines uv vers,
Bevore I came across en, you would av erd me swear an curse,

I never took to writing twud take me var to lung,
Thain this yer new vangeld word processor, append to come alung.

Caw yer, tez eh proper job, tez amazen what ee'll do,
Ee prints letterz, lung, zhort, wide an smaw, thain zaves et all vor you.

Mind you I got me trubles wain, the spull checker ez riged up rung,
I'm tell'n ee now, I did'n put up with thick thing very lung.

Whain ever I rawt a zimple word, like nort, or baint or dree,
The darn thing made this vunny noise, twoud drive ee maze you zee.

Me wive zhe cept conplainen, cuz er coud'n get to slaap,
All the time I wuz usin en, er erd thiz blaap! blaap! blaap!

Vuzt time that er 'erd en, zhe thought the microwave wuz on the blink.
Yer you can laf, but I tell'ee tez a lot more annoyen than you think.

At vinizh I got Denzil, to come an av a look,
Ee zaid, "The way thay'v got en programed, you'd never write a book!"

Us viddled weh the works a bit, an switched the zpull check off,
Now ee rins zo quiete, wull I can yer the youngsters cough.

Zo there et ez, I'v rung up Mr CANON to come an av a look,
But eez taken zo darn lung to come, I zhall av vinizhed the bloomen book . . .

SHOUD US KAPE A COW

ଏଓଽଏଓଽଏଓଽଏଓଽ

Mary me missez er kept pesteren me to buy er a cow,
But I knew I'd av to mulk et, cuz er did'n knaw ow.

I coud make me awn budder an us ud zave pounds on mulk,
Zhe wanted a Jursey, weh pansy eyes an a cawt like zulk.

"**D**o'ee knaw wat tez like to mulk a cow night en mornen,
Me zetten under er, while yu'm still een bade znoren."

Zhe zaid, "You can titch me to mulk, an I'll look adder er,"
I wuz thinken uv vood an the vencen, an the cost I'd incur.

Us argued zum more, but I new er ud ween,
Thain er started, pleaden "please Tam" weh that I gave een.

"**T**ez zilly ver me to gev eento'ee like this," I zes,
I bet yu'al be zorry, whain you zeez all the mud an the mess,

The vollo'n Tuesday us went of to Atherleigh,
Twaz best market to go, but I'd av to bid carevully.

Tez a lovely old market you can buy anything there,
Gozlens ducks, gawts, banties, or even a chiar.

An most uv the characters there, ez uv a dyen breed,
They come een lung cawts, dirdy wellys, an zcarvs over their 'ade.

They'ed ztan their all day, to zell dree muscovie ducks,
Thain peddow 'ome ten mile, they did'n drave trucks.

Us walked up drew the cows to zee if us vancied any,
Mother zaw wan er liked, but I thought erd make to much money.

Be the zize uv er udder, us ud av to carry er mulk on a trolley!
I ad me misgivens, an wuz zure that us ud zoon knaw our volly.

At last er appeared een the ring, the cow Mary lung to av,
Auctionier zays "here's a vine looking cow vour a day, an een cav".

I bid up to eighty vore er, an thought that wuz enough,
But missez thought otherwize, an got een eh uf.

I bid wance more, just az 'ammer wuz droppen,
Mary looked weh a zmile, a thank'ee ver not stoppen.

On thick bid, Mary waz the awner uv a vine Juresey cow,
I zpoze also, thick bid ad stoped us vrom 'aven a row.

Whain us got'er back 'ome, wich wuz about vive o clock,
Zhe were introdused to the cat, the dug an vew uther stock.

Now wuz the time ver Mary to av er vuz lezzon,
I told er, zh'ed be all right az lung ez erd lizten,

Us ad a'bit uv'a struggel tie'n cow up,
Zhe tossed up er ade an bumped Mary on lep.

I told er, zit on er right zide, an 'old a tit at left an right corner,
Now squaze vrom the top, then ztart again at the vormer.

Zhe got zwiped een the eye weh a wet dirty tale,
Thain the cow twice, put er vut een the pail.

Mary looked a'bit vlushed, I coud zee er wuz breathen vire,
Zhe did'n zay much cuz twer zhe, ooz idia twaz, to buy'er,

I though et best ver me to leave Mary to et,
The way er wuz looken, the bucket er might dro'et!

I'll zay this ver Mary though, er woud'n give een,
Back een the kitchen I gave the ztrainer an mulk pan a clain.

Whain zhe vinally got back to the 'ouse, I zays, "Knew ee woud'n vail,"
Weh a zmirk on er vase, er zaid, "I need another pail" . . .

༅༈༅༈༅༈༅༈

VARMER 'CROSS THE VALLEY

ෂාගුෂාගුෂාගු

Ee's wan uv they up country chaps, weh collage education,
Oow comes down yer weh rubber gloves, vull of expectation.

The zilly dope az left good zoil, deep well drained an loamy,
Us knaw the varm ee's varming now, wull, where tisn't clay, tiz stoney!

Ee's bought a brand new tractor, car and truck as wull,
Juz where ee gets eez money vrom, at thiz time tiz 'ard to tull.

Jim tawd me only t'uther day, ee zaw a oss drinking en eez streem,
Ee zaid, "et wernt a liddle wan," in vact twaz the bigest ee ad zeen.

Next thing ee'll be of to racez tryen to keep up weh nobz,
They zay ee got a ossey wive, oow'z given Jane an Mary jobz.

The mizzez came 'ome vrom zhoppin. zhe'd met this ossey type,
zhe zaw er buyin vancy vruit en veg, mother nearly droped er tripe.

"I don't knaw ow they do et" er zaid, while er wuz vinizhin up er mash,
"I struggle zcrimp, scrape, en zave, an er weh all that cash."

An now ave ee 'aerd the latest? they'm gwain on oliday!
"Yea Greeze I think er zaid it wuz, comen back a wick next Zaterday."

Thiz ez getten quite a scandall, av ee ever 'erd the like,
vancy gwain off on oliday "a varmer!" Wull tez never right!

Gallivanting off like that, lave'n zome wan elze to do es work,
I'll bet ee wan poun to zhillen, that ee we'ill ver zertain lose eez zhirt! . . .

ෂාගුෂාගුෂාගු

SWEDE PULLER GRADE 1

ഌരഌരഌരഌര

I'll tell'ee uv times whain ee ad to work 'ard all day,
Whain zhearin an zwede pullen wuz the only thing that ud pay.

By'gad it were ard, you'd work till twaz dark,
Av a quick baf, zupper an bade, then up weh the lark.

Zwede pullen ver all you that dawn't understand,
Iz pullen zwede out, then choppen leaves off weh ook een t'uther 'and

Now on this yer morning, us ad a new bloke ver to start,
Ee talked real posh, a proper bright spark.

Us zat een the van weh leggens an mack,
wachen en take iz things out eez zack.

Ee ad a zallad all made nice on a plaet,
An put et down carefull like, right next to the gaet.

Us zaid, "Ee'l av to watch that, whain thick tractor et's thick puddle!
Or whain Jan lets iz dug out the van ver iz piddle!"

Twas gwain a be a vun day, twaz easy to tull,
specially whain us got warmed up, pulling like ell.

Vus thing ee doo'z, wuz go strait to middow of vee-old,
An starts pullen like mad, but naw zwedes ud yield.

Us zhouted, "Ow do'ee think us coud get to they zwedes,
Weh out skwaten the good wanz een to liddow beeds!"

Ee thinks the varmer got a elicopter weh grabs,
An takes em back to the varm een drabs.

Us started to laf at thiz yer zity bloke,
Twaz turnen out to be wan ella'v joke.

Back at the gaet us told'n to start at the edge,
An work round the vee-old to make a wide ledge.

Weh plumb een iz mouth ee zaid "I will soon learn,
Well I'm bound to! I've got ten 0 levals!" made us squirm.

Us looked across an winked at wan t'uther,
Jan zaid, "way ee's 'olden thick ook, ee'l zoon av another,"
Hooooo!!....

Us wached ver awile to zee ow eed go,
Ee zeamed to be tryen waven ez ook to en vrow.

But twaz no good, you coud'n vind ez zwedes,
Ee ad em buried under vive tons of leaves.

Us told'n twaz "leaves to the left, an zwedes to the right,"
Jan wanned to tell'n rung, But I woud'n av spite.

Mind you, they were liddow beggers to get out the groun,
I reckend wance roun the vee-old, and ee'd be 'omeward boun.

But ee struggled on, an I zpoze ee did'n do zo bad,
I'll tell'ee ver nort thaw, you coud'n ate eez zallad!!..

JACK LUCKMEN

Jack Luckmen ad the zlowest drawl I'v yerd een the Deb'n tongue,
Ee ad a zon oow whain born, measured tweny nine inches lung.

"A yard en af uv pump water," that's what Mother zaid at the time,
About nine stone een weight an zix voot vive taw, at the age uv twenty nine.

The Luckmenz wuz our neighbours 'bout thirty yer ago,
I can mind the lung winded conversation'z en zayen to Dad, "Let's go."

Wance whain us wuz maken the boundry 'edge Jack comm'd up to yap,
I wuz twelve yer old an zhawen off, I zwung the axe, an a limb vell weh a znap.

Jack zaid, "Yer, . . can't . . your . . biy zwing . .
an . . axe, . . . ,ee . . chopped . . . thick . . . limb . .
right . . drew . . . . . ,"
I erd Dad zay, "my stud vee ez vive underd poun,"
Oh Jack ad a liddow chew.
Then zaid, "Zpose... tez... good... idea... to
kape.. vee.. up... midlin,... then.. you...
woud'n.. get... zo.. much.. to.. do."

Wull, ee can imagine, what twaz like ver me,
listen'en to that all adder noon,
Whain twaz time to go 'ome ver tay, I tell'ee
twud'n be none to zoon.

ಸಂಕ್ಷೇಪಂಕ್ಷೇಪ

VUS DAY UV ZHEAREN

ಊಆಊಆಊಆಊಆ

If I thought zwede bashen were 'ard I ant erd the last,
Learnen to zhear a zheep woud drive'ee af daft.

My vus day uv learnen wuz een a nizzen ut,
Right at the back weh no winda an the door af zhut.

The vooms vrome the injin woud give ee ade ake,
And the noise and rattoes, wull you coud'n yer yer zell spake.

The zheep they were scronny and woolly az ell,
Weh dung and piddow makin an ella'v smell.

Dennis me mate; ood zheard zeveral bevore,
Wuz zhearin where ee coud get zum air, nearer the door.

Ee zaid "Mind ee don't cut um, or varmer'al av'ee bard."
I picked up the clippers, and knew twuz gwain a be 'ard.

Catchen a zheep an zitten en on the vloor,
All this yer wool, what next wuz een store?

Gwain down iz belly, I wuz do'n all right,
But whain I went lower the begger took vrite!

Ee jumped an ee reggald right out me 'and,
Runnen drue me legs and under injin stan.

Zee'n all this zcummer the varmer ee started to stare,
en Dennis ee looked acrozz an zaid "I thought you did'n zwear!"

My back it wuz aken, and me 'andz were getten zore,
I velt like given up an just zit on the vloor.

The dug started barken, and the zheep began to stir,
The varmer zhouted at'n, "go back go back, come yer come yer".

Tez vunny ow varmers ull zhout at their dugs,
Cuz adder awile you can tull tiz the dug that they luves.

Weh back ake'n like ell I zheard zixteen more,
Twaz twenty to ten weh the light getten poor.

I ad zheard all day an I ad'n cut any,
Back 'ome weh the wive, er zaid, "av'ee zheard manny?"

"**Z**eventeen" I zaid, zhe zaid, "Iz that all"
"What' do'e mean?" I zez, "can you zhear any at'aw"?

Zhe looked a bit mad an got a'bit prickly,
"Hu" zhe zays, "There's a women een Australia oow zhears a underd an zixty"!

☙☙☙☙

ZCWIB'S TORCH

ಸಿಧಿಸಿಧಿಸಿಧಿಸಿಧಿ

This ez a zimple story, 'bout why Zcwib ad bought a torch,
Eee tawd me all about et, while us wuz ztanden een the porch.

Now zome may zay that Zcwib, waz not relly quite all there,
Ee 'eld ee'z ade to wan zide, an ad a vunny stare.

But ee waz all-uz very vrendly, an reliable weh the ztock
Us worked alung, zide be zide, I liked en quite eh lot.

Any ow, about the torch, ee'd bought'n to take teh pub,
Ee'd go every zaterday night, ver a pint an a bit eh grub.

Apparently whain gwain 'ome at night, pedlen down
Morch Rawd straight,
The cars on vull beem woud dazzle en, Zcwib got een eh state.

Ee 'ad a liddow vlazh light, zo ee coud zee where ee waz gwain,
But ee thought ee'd buy a biger wan, then ee coud play em at
zame game.

Zcwib zaid "It really works a trate, you zhoud zee em swerv,
En vact last zaterday night, wan drove up on the kerb."

Zo there ee waz zhowen me iz torch, twaz about eighteen
enchess lung,
Ee zaid it 'old's nine batteriez, weh thiz you can't go rung.

Ee zaid it's unbreakable, and drew et on the vloor,
Poor Zcwib, I thought I waz gwain eh laf, an av to zhut the door.

Ee'd scrimped an zaved an worked lung hours, and all that money voun,
Ee went quite ray'd an I zaw thick stare, the torch waz een pieces on the groun.

Zo there ee stood like een a trance, ee looked zo broken 'arted,
Next zaterday night ee'd be blinded again, right back where ee started!

ಌಌಌಌಌಌ

CHAPEL

Whain I wuz ten wich ez a lung time ago,
Us ad to go to chapel an etten Zunday Zkuel.

An un evry Vriday night, us ud go ver an hour,
To learn ow to rezite, an zing een the quire.

Becuz I wuz big, ver orgen, I pumped air,
En cuz uv where 'andow wuz, the wall I'd stair.

There wuz zounds uv ruzhen weend, an the 'andow squaaked,
En the organist's chair made noises, whain the stopperz er rayched.

The ticher an orgenist wuz both Mrs Monday,
Ver all vour yerz I went, er did'n mizz a Zunday.

Us liked er a'lot, vrom all mischief er zeamed ammoon,
I'll tell'ee ver nort thaw, er zung way out uv toon.

Twaz a mile to chapel an I walked weh Gwenny,
Zhe wuz me girl vriend, bevour er, I ad'n ad any.

On the way 'ome I'd call een at garage ver paraffin, ver lamps,
Then stan under Oke weh Gwenny, till me 'and got the cramps.

Why I did'n put thick can down, I zhall never knaw,
Gwenny must av thought me ella'v slaw.

Us woud stan ver af'our then kiss weh eh bump,
I'd rin down the rawd, villen a right blimmen chump.

Twaz on a Zunday zkuel outen that I lost er to another,
Eez vather ad a bigger varm, an ee'ad a big brither.

Wance a yer there woud be a big annual zervice,
The chapel'd be vull, een the iles an evry crevice.

Us ud zit in the vront vacen the congregation,
Waiten till twaz our turn to zay our rezetation.

Pritcher would be old, an spake brauder Deb'n than me.
This wan, the way ee wuz squinten, I'd zwear ee couden zee.

"What av'ee all come yer vouwer ___", ee'd zhout vrom the pulpit,
"To open up yer 'arts an pray to God", I started giglin, now I woud coppit.

Mrs Boundy een vront raw, wuz wipen zum spit away,
Er got ett een the eye, whain ee'd shouted, " 'art's an pray"

I coud zee Mother getten emotional, az the zermen dragged on,
I knew vrom experience, that wance more to the Lord erd belong.

Thain zure-nuf, weeping, down the vront er came,
Me veelen embarrazzed, every yer twaz the zame.

I knew ver the next vew wicks, erd luv us an 'old,
But adder to wicks of be'en that good, erd axplode.

Now twaz our turn to zay our pice an pervorm,
Us ud spake right loud, smaw wans, ud stan on a vorm.

Me dree yer old brither, wuz star over us lot,
Pritcher tawd congregation, ee wuz cherry on top.

Zo that's ow ett wuz all they yers ago,
I ztill baint a christian, but stons, I won't drowe.

Tez wizdom us all needs, an this 'elped me get ett,
Zo I'll leave et that, but I we-ill never verget ett. . .

༄༅༄༅༄༅

BROTHER'S PRIDE

ಌಯಌಯಌಯಌಯ

I tull of dree brithers I got to knaw, while zhearin zheep,
Dree real old bachelors, they varmed two underd acres, most uv et steep.

I ad all-uz wonered why they appeared zo dignivied an proud,
Cuz if they din'n zee the zhambles, wull their 'ade wuz een clouds.

They muzt uv been a vair age between zixty an zeventy,
Whain us arived to do zhearen, there'd all-uz be'u calamity.

There were slates een the rawd an vencen wuz poor,
Zheep ud escape, an rin right back to the moor.

Old Ben coud walk vive mile an 'our, althaw ee wuz zhort,
Ee'z wellies ud be vair vlopen, an ee'd be off weh a znort.

Ben all-uz looked all wellies, vunny old chap;
I mine ee'd kape eez backie tin under eez cap.

Ee ad liddow peg eye's an a ruddy gert noze,
An a pack uv cards een iz pocket, zhowen women een nude poze.

I never took much notice uv what I call, middow wan uv the dree,
Can't mine eez name, but ee wiz the wan oow made tay.

Len the boss, oow rin the varm, wuz really quite civilised,
But obviouzly coud'n cope, thaw I don't think ee realised.

The narra cobbled yard ad piles uv dung ten voot 'igh,
An big ramblin varm ouze wuz juz like a pegs sty.

Thain quite be chanse I happend acrozz the raizin ver their pride,
I looked drew barn door, an biggest bull I'd ever zead wuz een zide.

I really ant zeed the like, et muzt uv weighed a ton or more,
Thain dree zheds alung twaz the zame, only this time a boar.

I thought to me zelv "What's the point uv that!?"
They'd be no good ver breeden, to eavy an vat.

Zo I azked old Ben, "What do ee do weh the bull?"
If you get'n much vater the barn wull be vull.

O Ben ee chuckled an zaid, "You 'aven't 'erd,?
Us take um to the big county zhaw, last yer us come third."

Zo that wuz the raizin they dree brithers looked zo proud,
They zurvived all yer lung zo they coud get acclaim vrom the crowd.

That wance a yer zhawen, an be'n zupreme,
Wuz blinden um vrom the mess, they wuz most zertainly een. .

ᏃᏣᏃᏣᏃᏣᏃᏣ

I'VE AD A BELLY VULL

ಬಂಡಬಂಡಬಂಡ

Dick Blackverd wuz Dad's neighbour many yers ago,
Now I'm talken way back, whain I wuz still gwain to zkuel.

Ee ad an awvull temper, ee'd cuz an go af mad!
An did'n elp thing's very much, zharen a boundry edge weh Dad.

Dad ad a bull, strong, young, uncivilised an vrisky,
Ee let et escape een the muddy lane, ee shoud uv knawd twuz risky.

Ee wached en go weh ade eld 'igh, bellowen, all the while,
Caw!, coud'n thick bull roar! ee zertenly went weh style.

Twaz getten late an almost dark, pointlezz to give chase,
An anyow it wer ver zertain, that Dad ud loose the race.

While gwain drew eez back door, on thick calm an tranquil night,
Dad erd the bull still trumpeting, more an af a mile out uv zight.

"Wull tez no good ver me to worry now, I'll wait 'tull the mornen,"
Twaz getten late nearly ten o clock, an Dad ad started yawnen.

Ee only ad wan voot on stairs, whain the vhone started ringen,
Twaz Dick Blackverd een a rage, my Gad! an won'ee zingen!

Ee cuzed an vumed, damned, blasphemed, you shoud av yerd the language,
Dad eld the vhone a voot vrom iz yer, incase et did zome damage.

Dad zaid, "There's nothen I can do tonight" Dick Blackverd started coughen,
Ee coughed zo much you'd think ee'd choke, Dad, I'm vrade, wuz laughen.

Whain the choken vinally stoped, ee zaid "You get this bloody bull!
Eez een our garden pawing stons, I'v ad a belly vull!!"

"Cant'ee yer the ztons ratlen gainst the door?
Now lizten Tom, I've ad enough, I zhant take any more!"

Dad zaid, "I av a problem, tez black ez ink out there,"
"Woud you vancey vazen a bull een the dark? I bet twoud make you stare!"

The reply wuz, "You get the bugger now, or I swear I'll shoot the zod!"
Dad zaid, "Dawn't be rash I'll do me best, thick bull cost a vair vew bob."

Dad went up to the local pub, to vind zome men weh torches,
Whain ee told em what the trouble wuz, they zeemed uneazy on their perches.

They zaid, "now Tom, us knaw nort uv bulls, us woud'n knaw where to start,"
"Tez no good Tom, don't azk us." They then drew another dart.

Twaz no point een tryen more, Dad ud 'ave to lave et 'tull the mornen.
Zo that what ee did ee went 'ome to bade, an een no time at all, wuz snoren.

But I'm avraid ver Dad it wernt over yet, zoon there wuz ammeren on our door,
This time twaz the zargent vrom the town, twaz midnight, an won'ee zore.

"**T**om, Dick Blackverds been on the vhone, an want's me to 'old up the law,"
"You'v got a bull, an eez cauzen stress, you knaw I 'ad to call."

Dad zaid, "If they stays en zide, they won't come to 'arm, I'll vech'en een the mornen,"
The zargent coud zee that Dad wuz stubborn, zo ee gave me Dad this warnen;

"**Y**ou knaw the rule, you keep a bull, you shoud kape en tied, or pend,"
"You could be liable ver damages, an av a zumons to devend!"

Zo zoon's twas light, Dad zet off, to zee if Billy done zome 'arm,
Ee voun en niblin hay, vrom eenzide, Dick Blackverd's barn.

Dad grabbed the rope zayen, "You'v ad your vun." Billy gave wan vinal roar.
Twaz az ef zo ee he wuz playzed to be off, en ee quietly came drew the door.

Dick Blackverd coud be zeen scwinten, vrom the corner of eez ouze,
An wached zheepishly az Billy waz led away, az dozile as a mouze.

A bit uv a anticlimax, zome of ee might zay.
But I tell'ee now; 'no wan' was more playzed than Dad, that Billy waz only niblen *hay!*.

<u>Voot Note</u>

I zpose thiz story waz az much about Dick Blackverd, az et waz about Dad's bull.
But wan thing I knaws ver zertain, Dick Blackverd, weh Dad, ad many more *belly vullz!!*

ALL-UZ ON A ZUNDAY

৸৻৶৸৻৶৸৻৶

Mum walked 'ome vrom chapel veelen quite refreshed,
But us kids knew by bade time erd be veelen wull distressed.

Cuz now again twaz Zunday, whain Dad became alive,
On Monday Tewzday Wedenzday, ez varmen ee'd let slide.

Why he made thiz day iz work day, I zhall never knaw,
Thaw twer all-uz me zuspicion, twaz cuz the vamily all-uz zhaw.

Mum woud start to make dinner, whain the zaw bench zhe woud yer,
You coud zee er leps visibly tighten, az er speeded up er stir.

The zaw et needed zharpening, Dad woud start another job.
Go and vetch the crozz-cut zon, there's a tree I'd like to lob.

Us'll take zome matchez weh uz, an you can burn the bracken on the 'ill,
I all-uz really liked this, et gave me zuch a thrill.

Vlamez woud raych vorty veet, and coud be zeed ver miles aroun,
Muther woud zurely zee em, they woud'n be 'idden by the moun.

Thain nighbourz woud come rinnen, worried about their vence,
If vlamez got really out uv control, I zpose the cost coud be immense.

But vather wuz zuch a rascal, he'd razzure em weh iz charm,
An us kids velt zafe az wull, he woud'n let us come to any 'arm.

Another Zunday ad rayched its culmination, vather'd gained a day for vree,
Now there wuz only wan big question, "Woud us be getten any tay?"

ಬಂಧಬಂಧಬಂಧ

ME OLD MAN'S DRAVEN

ഌരഌരഌരഌര

Vrum the age uv vourty vive you coud blame me ver the way me vather drove,
I wuz only dree yers old an left a bag uv stones een ez rawd.

Walken drue the pump ouze juz bevore dark,
Weh a bucket een wan and, en een t'uther a vark,

Dad went ass over tip an landed on a scraper,
The andow et ez eye, et zwauld up like a tater.

Ee ad to go to doctos oow zaid, "yul never zee zu wull",
I still veels gulty whain I think uv ow me vather vull.

I toden to keep over whain with'n I'd ride,
Ee'd drive over to the right, an waeve to the rung zide.

The carz cummen t'uther way woud look een dizbelief,
Me whain car got by zafe' I ad this velen uv relief.

Tiz nothen zhort uv a mirrical now at the age uv zemty vive,
That adder draven all they miles, that ee ez still alive.

I vollowed en 'ome vrom market only dree months ago,
Twaz ee'n the middow uv winter an ee wuz draven een the snaw.

Me, I wuz strugglen weh the weel to keep my car en controw!
But ee, I don't think ee even realized the rawd wuz vull uv snaw!

But now tez got beyond a joke, ver ez mind iz gone zume what,
Last wick ee drove right by ee'z ouze dree nights on the trot.

ಬಂಡಬಂಡಬಂಡ

DANCEN

Een the vifties, me an mate Arold used zycle to dance's,
Ee'z bike ad Ztermy Archers gears, mine wuz ex vorce's.

Et weigh'd af a'ton, en darn thing wuz ella'v low geard,
I ad to peddow like ell to keep up, or Arold disappeared.

If I tawd Dad I wanned a bike, I'd aind up weh vour,
Whain ee went to the market ee'd call een at ex army store.

Thain adder the ex army store, t'woud be Bervells zecond 'and zhop,
Dad ud pick out a zuit, zhirt an tie, en barter weh a vew poun uv crame, ver the lot.

Zo there I'd be, weh me army bike an me zecon 'and clauths,
Dree bob een me pocket, greaze on me turnups, wanderen if et zhaws.

We'd av wan zhellen left adder us ad paid to get een,
Us ud stan at the rear, zhoulders back arms volded an belly pulled een.

Girls ud be zat roun the hall on chiars,
An a vew 'um wuz dancen together een pairs.

Twud take a brave vella, to be vuzt on the vloor,
You'd av to be pretty zerten erd stan up, that's ver zure.

But that did'n evect us, cuz us coud'n dance,
Ver another two yers us stood, een our regular stance.

Us coud zee girls zuspenders, wain they danced the walz,
An us coud av zworn, that what they ad under their blouse's wuz valz.

Then twuz time ver revreshments, ver wan zhellen us coud buy a zamwedge en tay,
And zume uv the ladies, drew een an extra zamwedge ver vree.

৪০৫৪৮০৫৪৮০৫৪৮০৫৪

DEATH ALLY

෩෬෩෬෩෬෩෬

I mine the time whain Dad took dree muzcovie ducks to market,
Ee never ad any cash you zee, the ducks wuz ow ee'd get et.

Ee wuz alright ver iz dinner, ver that ee'd zwop zome crame,
The lady at the chip shop woud take et weh a gleam.

I'd be zat there all awkward like, while Dad did the deal,
Thain zure enough vive minutes later, Dad woud come back weh the meal.

Naw: the ducks wuz to buy the petrol, ver the jurney gwain 'ome,
Ee only ad enough to travel wan way, an that drop wuz on loan.

Whain Dad vineshed looken ver zomethin chaap, roun the peg pens an the like,
(Any bargains) ee'd pay ver next wick, or zhoud zay; "ee might!"

Ee'd call een at the butchers zhop, car all ready spluttering,
Dad walked towards the butchers, muzcovie ducks vair vluttering.

Zhoppers woud be starin, wull twaz right een middow of town!
Dad shawed em to the butcher, you zhoud uv zeed the vrown.

If yu'm wan of they them skweamizh types, you may not want to raad more,
But all thiz yer append over vourty yers ago, whain volk's were very poor.

Butcher zaid, "Can't take em like that! they must be plucked an daid,"
You may not beleive thiz, but Dad vound a liddow ally way, I don't knaw where it led.

But af an hour later, vrom thick ally, vather reappeared,
Olden dree daid muzcovie ducks, every veather cleard!.

Never did vind out what append to the veathers, or where thick ally went,
But can still zee Dad an the butcher laughing now: az these vew words I vent. . .

REUBIN'S LAMENT

ಸಂಲಿಸಂಲಿಸಂಲಿಸಂಲಿ

I worked vourty yers ver old varmer Hammen,
An retired last yer weh a gift uv a zalmon.

Reccon my avridge wage ver they vourty yers,
Wuz dree pounz a wick, twoud bring ee to tears.

Varmer Hammen ee preached at the chapel, an ad a big car,
Ee wuz iley respekted by vokes near an var.

Adder workin vourty yers a zalmon wuz the best ee coud do,
Vourty yers, uv blood an zweat and all-uz be'n true.

But that's ow live ez I triez not to be bitter,
T'wouden be zo bad if I velt a'bit vitter.

Thaw I av got me cottage an dree acres uv groun,
Did'n ever marry, cuz there wuz naw good women aroun.

I live all way up 'ill, on edge uv Pauwson moor,
Me nearest neighbours vive miles away, or more.

I've got me dug an me cat I can talk to if I want,
I can't do weh these volkes weh cars an money to vlaunt.

Every great market day, wich ez wance u mounth,
I goes een Molton ver a pint, an buy's me zell lunch.

Last time I wuz een I advertised zum puppy's ver zale,
There's dree uv litter left, two dark and wan pale.

A vew days ago, a cuppow come up vrom town,
They did'n like the pale wan, an ad the best brown.

I thought I'de be vrendly an zhaw em me stock,
Two cows an oss, an vive zheep, not enough ver a vlock.

I told um their names an all the abbits they ad,
An ow wan uv the zheep wuz a liddow bit mad.

They looked to be enterested they smiled a lot,
But whain they drove down the rawd, I new twaz all rot.

Ver whain I walked to the car an zhut the girls door,
The winder wuz a'bit down, an I erd er zay what an old bore.

The 'airs on me neck got a bit prickly,
They zaw that I erd, an drove away quickly.

Another day gone an all the ztock vaid,
Vealin a'bit down I went of to bade.

Next mornen wuz zuny whain I let the dugs out,
Then vrome boddum ov drive, I erd the postman zhout.

Ee zaid, "Av'ee erd, old man Hammens died! an every wans een mournen!"
Veeden me zheep I thought, "What a bewdevull mornen!"

৪০৫৪০৫৪০৫৪০৫

TEZ ONLY TEMPORARY

ಏಃಬಃಏಃಬಃಏಃಬಃಏಃಬ

"That'll do ver now, tez only temporary, us'll vinish that tomorrow,"
Vather ud all-uz leave a job af done, an did'n et caus zome zorrow.

Us ad temporary vences, roovs, doors, an chairs,
There wuz even a vour inch nail, kapen up the stairs.
(Twaz only Temporary)

The pegs broke een to neighbours, an rooted up iz grass,
Neighbour wuz zo bad tempered, ee zaid ee'd kick Dad's ass!

Vather'd repaired the 'edge, weh a piece of rotten plank,
If peg enjoyed the neighbours roots, wull, ee ad me Dad to thank.
(Twaz only Temporary)

Ee made an ark ver zow to slaap, good dezign an een proportion,
But whain zow went to rub er back, wull, I'd call et demolition!

Ee vixed a door to out 'ouze, to protect against the weather,
Ee only ad wan 'inge you zee, zo he used a bit uv leather.

Then there wuz the time ee lost a ztud, vrom wheel uv the car,
Ee only ad to drave to village zhop, twaz'nt very var.

Dad ee ad brainwave, ee'd only use dree ztuds, instead uv putten vour,
Wheel came off an 'it a wall, an bounced right drew the bake'ouze door.
(Twaz only Temporary)

Don't get the rung impression, now eez gone us mizzez 'im a'lot,
An realize that een they days, you either ad money to do the job, or not.

Yez ee past away nerly ten yer ago, us all veel very zad,
Zo on end uv grave, these words us rawt
"Tez only Temporary Dad."

DEB'N DIALECT VERSE

☙❧☙❧☙❧

I've rawt Dialect verse that's zound'z very rhythmical.

Tried to concoct verse that's 'appy and muzical.

Zome 'av zaid "this verse ez quite educational."

A lot of verse I've rawt iz now unretractable.

I got vair exzited whain a vella zaid "Thiz verse iz classical."

An to tell a vunny story, wull verse iz very practical.

I rawt a verse the t'uther day, twaz zo bad twaz laughable.

Then there wuz the verse I rawt, vicar zaid wuz unvorgivable.

You can zee the abbit uv writing verse ez really quite incurable.

But to try an write zome dialect verse that zoundz poetical,

I woud like to put on record now, iz bloody nigh ***impossible!!***

☙❧☙❧☙❧

GLOSSARY

adder	after	ee'll	he'll
af	half	ee'd	he'd
abit	habit	en	in/him
a'be	to be	erd	heard she'd/her'd
'and	hand	eez	his
ad	had	ee'ad	he had
ade	head	etten	attend
'art	heart	een	in
'ard	hard	gawts	goats
av	have	geat (gee'at)	gate
av'ee	have you	gwain	going
all-uz	always	iz	is
althaw	although	juz	just
ant	haven't	knaw	know
an	and	naw	no
awn	own	kape	keep
bade	bed	kiln	kill it
baint	am not	lave	leave
brithers	brothers	laf	laugh
boddum	bottom	liddow	little
boun	bound	middow	middle
by gad	my goodness	mouwth	mouth
clauths	clothes	mine	remember
cuz/cauz	because	mulk	milk
coud'n	couldn't	narra	narrow
dawn't	don't	naice	nice
dree	three	nort	nothing
did'n	didn't	o'den	hold it
drew	threw/through	ook	hook
drow	throw	'ome	home
ella'v	hell of a	oss	horse
ee	he	oow	who

43

pegs	pigs	vrum	from
playzed	pleased	vine	fine
plait	plate	vront	front
proper	excellent/lovely	vloor	floor
rayched	reached	vella	fellow
rayzen	reason	vancey	fancy
raw	row (as in line)	vacin	facing
rawt	wrote	vair	really
rung	wrong	vew	few
smouw	smell	vunny	funny
thaw	though	voun'en	found it
tawd	told	voun	found
thain	then	vull	full
tez	it is	vuz/vuzt	first
tuln	tell him	wan	one
thick	that	wain	with it
tweny	twenty	weh	with we
trate	treat	wick	week
thicky	that one	wuz	was
tull'ee	tell you	wun'ee	wasn't he
t'uther	the other	yu'm	you are
twaz	it was	yer	here/ear/hear
t'wouden	it would'nt	zmaw	small
ud twoud	would/it would	zpull	spell
ulp	help	zpecially	especially
underd	hundred	zkwatin	squashing
uz'll	we will	zpoze	suppose
voun	found	zeed	seen/seed
uv	of	zlaep	sleep
ouze	house	zame	same
vee-old	field	zwauld	swollen
ver	for	zitty	city
voot	foot	zcummer	chaos
vree	free	zulk	silk
vriend	friend	z	s